Treasure Hunt

Lorinda Bryan Cauley

G. P. Putnam's Sons New York

G. P. Putnam's Sons, a division of The Putnam & Grosset Group,
200 Madison Avenue, New York, NY 10016.
G. P. Putnam's Sons, Reg. U.S. Pat. & Tm. Off.
Published simultaneously in Canada
Printed in Hong Kong by South China Printing Co. (1988) Ltd.
Designed by Patrick Collins
Text set in Horley Old Style Semibold

Library of Congress Cataloging-in-Publication Data
Cauley, Lorinda Bryan.   Treasure hunt/Lorinda Bryan Cauley.   p.   cm.
Summary: A rhyming treasure hunt where clues in each verse lead the reader through the
illustrations to a surprise ending. [1. Treasure hunts—Fiction.   2. Stories in rhyme.]   I. Title.
PZ8.3.C3133Tr   1994   [E]—dc20   93-14043   CIP   AC   ISBN 0-399-22447-5

1   3   5   7   9   10   8   6   4   2

First Impression

For Raul, Sophie, and Carmen

A treasure hunt—today's the day.
Come on in and you can play!

A surprise is waiting just for you
if you can follow every clue.

My favorite chair, a quiet nook—
Look for the clue inside a book.

A cozy place for a sleepy head—
The clue is under something red.

Coats and pants and sweaters, too—
Find the clue in a funny shoe!

A toy that whistles when you wind it—
Look inside and you will find it.

Rub-a-dub-dub, get squeaky clean!
The clue is under something green.

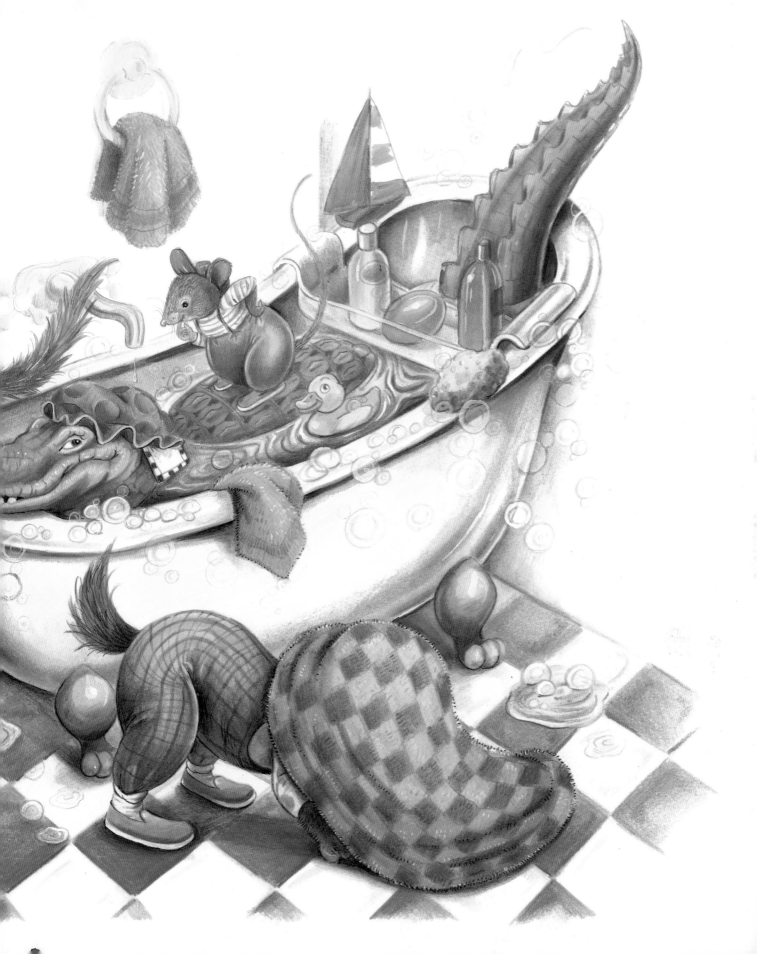

Where you cook and where you eat—
It's underneath my favorite treat!

You need one of these on a rainy day
before you can go out and play!

Open the door and out we go...
where corn and peas and carrots grow.

Splish! Splash! In jumps a frog—
You'll find a clue beneath a log.

Look in the branches, high and low,
where crunchy munchy apples grow.

In the clearing, in the wood—
Take a peek! It's something good!

Congratulations, everyone!
Come on in and have some fun!